MW00572500

PRAYERS & PROMISES
FOR
Grief
and Loss

BroadStreet
PUBLISHING

CONTENTS

INTRODUCTION

Everyone experiences difficult seasons in life. Loss,
pain, sickness, doubt, and loneliness can lead to
discouragement or a feeling of hopelessness.

Prayers & Promises for Grief and Loss is a topically
organized collection that guides you through themes
of assurance, compassion, inspiration, comfort, and
more. Encouraging Scriptures, heartfelt prayers, and
prompting questions give you an opportunity to think
more deeply about the hope found in God's Word.

God is the best source of comfort you will find. He
knows your heart and he is full of understanding for
every situation. Let his strength be yours as you cry out
to him. Bask in the calming peace of his presence and
take comfort in knowing that he will always be with you.

ABANDONMENT

"The Lord himself goes before you and will be with you;
he will never leave you nor forsake you."

Deuteronomy 31:8 NIV

The Lord loves justice and fairness;
he will never abandon his people.
They will be kept safe forever.

Psalm 37:28 TLB

God has said,
"I will never fail you. I will never abandon you."
So we can say with confidence,
"The Lord is my helper,
so I will have no fear."

Hebrews 13:5-6 NLT

"I will not abandon you as orphans—
I will come to you."

John 14:18 NLT

Lord, you have called me by name and I am yours. In the midst of suffering, knowing that you are my perfect Father fills me with peace. You meet me in my mess every time; I don't have to hide from you! Thank you for loving me so completely. I find hope in the promise that you will never abandon me or leave me to sort things out on my own.

When I struggle to see the light in the middle of the darkness of my circumstances, draw closer, Holy Spirit. Surround me with the embrace of your love and whisper your comforting words straight to my heart again. Like a mother's lullaby soothes her child, so lull my heart into peace as I lean into you. Calm my heart again in your presence.

How would you face today differently if you were absolutely convinced that God would never leave you?

ABILITY

"My grace is sufficient for you, for my power is made perfect in weakness." Therefore I will boast all the more gladly of my weaknesses, so that the power of Christ may rest upon me.

2 CORINTHIANS 12:9 ESV

After you have suffered for a little while, the God of all grace, who called you to His eternal glory in Christ, will Himself perfect, confirm, strengthen and establish you.

1 PETER 5:10 NASB

Take a new grip with your tired hands and strengthen your weak knees. Mark out a straight path for your feet so that those who are weak and lame will not fall but become strong.

HEBREWS 12:12–13 NLT

We are not saying that we can do this work ourselves. It is God who makes us able to do all that we do.

2 CORINTHIANS 3:5 NCV

Gracious God, you are so loving. Your strength is my source when I have no resources of my own left. Your Word says that your power is perfected in weakness; may I find this to be true in my life! When I am weak, then I am really strong because I am leaning into your power that is beyond anything I could muster up. While the rest of the world is bragging about their strengths, may I not fall into that trap. Instead, may I revel in the power you give in my weakness.

I am so limited, Lord. What a mystery that in your kingdom that actually is a benefit! Keep my heart humble in your presence that I would glory in your grace made evident in my life. Have your way in my frailty today.

Do you believe that God can
make you able to do what he asks?

ACCEPTANCE

"The Father gives me the people who are mine.
Every one of them will come to me,
and I will always accept them."

JOHN 6:37 NCV

The LORD does not see as man sees;
for man looks at the outward appearance,
but the LORD looks at the heart.

1 SAMUEL 16:7 NKJV

If God is for us, who can be against us?

ROMANS 8:31 ESV

Before he made the world, God chose us to be his very
own through what Christ would do for us; he decided
then to make us holy in his eyes, without a single fault—
we who stand before him covered with his love.

EPHESIANS 1:4 TLB

Lord, I come to you with my life again today. You said that you wouldn't cast out the one who moves toward you, so I trust that you welcome me in with your love. It doesn't matter how little or how much time has passed, you are still as warm in your acceptance of me as you were the first time I was met with your mercy. I won't hold anything back from you today.

There are no exceptions to your wonderful love; you always reach out in kindness. There is no debt or failure that you can't more than meet with your mercy. You are skillful in restoration and unstoppable in redemption. I know that as I look to you, I will see how you are weaving your faithful care through even the most terrible situations. Here's my heart, open before you. Heal me with your kindness and restore my hope in your affection.

Are you convinced that God
will never turn you away?

ANXIETY

LORD, you are my shield,
My wonderful God who gives me courage.
I can lie down and go to sleep, and I will wake up again,
Because the LORD gives me strength.
Thousands of troops may surround me,
but I am not afraid.

PSALM 3:3, 5-6 NCV

"Don't let your hearts be troubled.
Trust in God, and trust also in me."

JOHN 14:1 NLT

Give all your worries to him,
because he cares about you.

1 PETER 5:7 NCV

I call out to the LORD when I'm in trouble,
and he answers me.

PSALM 120:1 NIRV

Holy One, I come to you today with every worry, burden, and anxiety. Some days they are quieter than others; other days the noise level is too loud to hear anything else. I know that I don't need to carry the weight of these on my own, and I am not responsible to mitigate every possible outcome in life. There are innumerable unknowns, but not one is a mystery to you!

Lord, you see the end from the beginning and every moment in between. Why would I continue to expend energy on assumptive possibilities when you offer me the peace of your all-knowing presence? I may not know what tomorrow holds, but you do. I will trust you, Lord; you can have all my worries! Give me the confidence that comes with your nearness. I know that you are with me.

Can you rest in the knowledge that
God sees what you cannot?

ASSURANCE

To him who is able to do immeasurably more than all we
ask or imagine, according to his power that is at work
within us, to him be glory...for ever and ever! Amen.

EPHESIANS 3:20–21 NIV

All of God's promises have been fulfilled in Christ
with a resounding "Yes!"

2 CORINTHIANS 1:20 NLT

I go to bed and sleep in peace,
because, LORD, only you keep me safe.

PSALM 4:8 NCV

These things I have written to you who believe in the
name of the Son of God, that you may know that you have
eternal life, and that you may continue to believe in the
name of the Son of God.

1 JOHN 5:13 NKJV

Lord, you are full of lovingkindness at every moment. Your mercy rushes like a full river from your heart. When I feel like my heart is breaking and there is no silver lining to be found, you pull me close into your compassion and keep me still in the center of your love. Even when I can't feel you, I know that you are near.

When I have run out of ways to ask for help or the energy to reach out again, you remain faithful to your limitless love and perfect nature. In your mercy, Lord, move in ways that I can't even imagine. Blow me away with your goodness and reveal yourself through your power at work in my life today. I wait on you.

How does believing God's promises
cause you to feel reassured?

AUTHENTICITY

"Remember this: If you have a lofty opinion of yourself and seek to be honored, you will be humbled. But if you have a modest opinion of yourself and choose to humble yourself, you will be honored."

MATTHEW 23:12 TPT

What should be our proper response to God's marvelous mercies? I encourage you to surrender yourselves to God to be his sacred, living sacrifices. And live in holiness, experiencing all that delights his heart. For this becomes your genuine expression of worship. Stop imitating the ideals and opinions of the culture around you, but be inwardly transformed by the Holy Spirit through a total reformation of how you think. This will empower you to discern God's will as you live a beautiful life, satisfying and perfect in his eyes.

ROMANS 12:1–2 TPT

Father of mercy, in my sorrow I let myself come undone in your presence. I couldn't hold myself together if I tried. You are patient to sit with me in my discomfort and hold me close in your compassion. You don't expect me to process the pain I'm experiencing quickly or move on from my sadness rooted in loss. You are the closest comfort I've ever known and relief to my soul.

When you support me with your unfailing affection, the strength of your love keeps me rooted in who you are and in who I am in you. As I am loved to life, even in my darkest moments, I lean into your example of boundless mercy. As I experience it, so will I be able to offer it. I trust that in your time, nothing will have been wasted. Use every bit of this and turn it into beauty beyond my imagining.

How do you see yourself?
How do you think God sees you?

BEAUTY

Your beauty should come from within you—
the beauty of a gentle and quiet spirit that
will never be destroyed and is very precious to God.

1 PETER 3:4 NCV

Hold on to wisdom and good sense.
Don't let them out of your sight.
They will give you life
and beauty like a necklace around your neck.
Then you will go your way in safety,
and you will not get hurt.

PROVERBS 3:21-23 NCV

I praise you because you made me
in an amazing and wonderful way.
What you have done is wonderful.
I know this very well.

PSALM 139:14 NCV

Constant One, when everything fades, you remain unchanging in glory and light. Your goodness does not have an end; there is no cap on your kindness. If loss does anything, it brings awareness to the limited scope of this life. There is immense sadness in the ending of things. But you don't wither and you don't fade. And you have said that there is eternal life beyond—an opportunity to experience beauty beyond measure with no limit.

My heart takes hope in your Word. In my grief, I am not hopeless. In the pain of separation, I am not without hope. But still, the sting of death is real. Today, direct my gaze toward your unfailing love that leads into everlasting life. Give me a glimpse of what is forever and what will never change. You are so much better than I can imagine, and still my heart longs for more.

How has the pain of loss affected your view of eternity?

BELIEF

"For God so loved the world that he gave his one and only
Son, that whoever believes in him shall not perish but have
eternal life. For God did not send his Son into the world
to condemn the world, but to save the world through him.
Whoever believes in him is not condemned."

JOHN 3:16, 18 NIV

To all who did accept him and believe in him
he gave the right to become children of God.

JOHN 1:12 NCV

Believe on the Lord Jesus Christ, and you will be saved.

ACTS 16:31 NKJV

"All things are possible to him who believes."

MARK 9:23 NASB

"Blessed are those who have not seen
and yet have believed."

JOHN 20:29 ESV

Unchanging One, my hopes are set on you. Everything that I desire is fleeting—my longings pass away, except for that which finds its home in you. Your love knows no limits, and it is this unfailing love that covers and carries me through every day of my life. Today, meet me with the mercy of your heart and love me to life. Let your light shine into the shadows of my soul, bringing clarity and peace.

In walking through grief and loss, the sting of death is real; I cannot pretend to not be gutted by the sorrow that mourning elicits. And yet, there is hope even in the grief. Though the awaiting reality of eternal life doesn't ease the separation of loss, it does bring hope to the journey of life. Lord, would you give me the peace that passes all understanding today as I set my eyes on you, the Eternal One?

Do you have the assurance of eternal life?

BLESSING

LORD, you bless those who do what is right.
Like a shield, your loving care keeps them safe.

PSALM 5:12 NIRV

Surely you have granted him unending blessings
and made him glad with the joy of your presence.

PSALM 21:6 NIV

"Even more blessed are all who hear the word of God
and put it into practice."

LUKE 11:28 NLT

Give praise to the God and Father of our Lord Jesus
Christ. He has blessed us with every spiritual blessing.
Those blessings come from the heavenly world. They
belong to us because we belong to Christ. God chose us to
belong to Christ before the world was created. He chose
us to be holy and without blame in his eyes. He loved us.

EPHESIANS 1:3-4 NIRV

Lord God, you are my covering. There is not one moment where you turn away or remove your presence from my life. Even when I cannot sense your nearness, you are close. You faithfully cover me with your compassion all the days of my life. Today, you see right where I am and exactly what I'm facing. Flood me with a fresh knowing, Lord, that you are not only with me but that you are also for me.

Your love is more endless than the drops of water in the earth's atmosphere. You never run out or run dry; there is always a drink to satisfy the thirsty soul. You are my steady hope, Lord, the one who faithfully fulfills all of his promises. Let your favor cover and keep me as I press into you on my most difficult days. Whatever comes, I draw my strength from your presence.

Have you reflected on the blessing of God's constant presence lately?

BOLDNESS

He proclaimed the kingdom of God
and taught about the Lord Jesus Christ—
with all boldness and without hindrance!

ACTS 28:31 NIV

If an army surrounds me, I will not be afraid.
If war breaks out, I will trust the LORD.

PSALM 27:3 NCV

Sinners run away even when no one is chasing them.
But those who do what is right are as bold as lions.

PROVERBS 28:1 NIRV

Let us come boldly to the throne of our gracious God.
There we will receive his mercy,
and we will find grace to help us when we need it most.

HEBREWS 4:16 NLT

Merciful Lord, I come with confidence before your throne of grace today. I won't hold back anything as I approach you. Here's my heart, open wide before you. Here's my life, Lord, I loosen my grip and invite you to do what only you can do and what I could only dream of doing. The seeds of life you sow in me are so much better than my measly attempts at control will ever produce.

You don't miss a beat. It doesn't matter how often or how little I turn my attention to you; your affection for me never wavers. What an amazing, merciful Father you are, that you always welcome me with open arms! I am undone by your loving attention every time I receive it. May my heart be ever attuned to you, and may I find my true identity in the reflection of your affection.

Are you convinced of God's unwavering love for you?

CHANGE

Look! I tell you this secret:
We will not all sleep in death,
but we will all be changed.

1 CORINTHIANS 15:51 NCV

He will take our weak mortal bodies and change them
into glorious bodies like his own, using the same power
with which he will bring everything under his control.

PHILIPPIANS 3:21 NLT

Jesus Christ is the same yesterday and today and forever.

HEBREWS 13:8 NIRV

I will not be afraid, because the LORD is with me.
People can't do anything to me.

PSALM 118:6 NCV

Jesus, you are constant in love and mercy. You who humbly laid down your throne in heaven and your life in love are the same gracious man that sits at the right hand of the Father today. Father, Son, and Spirit are unified and perfect in mercy and love. As I look to your life, Jesus, I find that you always pursued the forgotten and were quick to call out truth instead of bias. You were not exclusive in who you chose to share your message of love with. You chose the normal to follow you not the religious elite.

Lord, as I follow after you, I am humbled to be yours. I am also relieved to know that you never expect perfection from me, and you certainly don't want me to pretend to be someone that I'm not. As I live my life in your presence, I continually find that you are transforming me to be more like you—to love more like you. May my heart be a sponge for your compassion and mercy, so when life squeezes me, your love would come out.

How do you handle change?

COMFORT

"God's dwelling place is now among the people,
and he will dwell with them....
'He will wipe every tear from their eyes.
There will be no more death' or mourning
or crying or pain."

May our Lord Jesus Christ himself and God our Father,
who loved us and by his grace gave us eternal comfort
and a wonderful hope, comfort you and strengthen you.

2 THESSALONIANS 2:16–17 NLT

Unless the LORD had helped me,
I would soon have settled in the silence of the grave.
I cried out, "I am slipping!"
but your unfailing love, O LORD, supported me.
When doubts filled my mind,
your comfort gave me renewed hope and cheer.

PSALM 94:17–19 NLT

Father, there is coming a day where there will be no more pain and no more weeping. I can hardly imagine that reality, and even more—I can hardly wait for it. Especially in the midst of deep grief, the thought of death being a distant memory is a hopeful one even if it feels far off and more wish-like than a coming reality.

One thing is for sure: you are always faithful. Your presence is like a seal of the promises you've made. Come and fill me with your powerful presence that changes me from the inside out. Comfort me with your tangible nearness and love. Encourage my heart today as I open myself to receive a fresh wave of your grace. Give me a taste of the coming goodness!

Does God's comfort in your present reality give you hope for the future fulfillment of his promises?

COMPASSION

When I am with those who are weak, I share their
weakness, for I want to bring the weak to Christ.
Yes, I try to find common ground with everyone,
doing everything I can to save some.

1 Corinthians 9:22 NLT

God, have mercy on me
according to your faithful love.
Because your love is so tender and kind,
wipe out my lawless acts.

Psalm 51:1 NIRV

Praise be to the God and Father of our Lord Jesus Christ,
the Father of compassion and the God of all comfort.

2 Corinthians 1:3 NIV

The Lord hears his people when they call to him for help.
He rescues them from all their troubles.

Psalm 34:17 NLT

Father, I will not hesitate to come to you with the reality of my heart today. I won't shrink back in fear, wondering if you will meet me with disapproval or with a smile of welcome. You are the perfect parent; you never turn away from your children with annoyance or disdain. You know me completely, and you accept me as I am.

Though I may question your intentions because of the experiences I've had with my own family, I know that you are so much better than anyone I've ever known. Your love is unrelenting in its intensity, without manipulation or expectation of certain conditions being filled. You fully embrace me in every state. You don't expect perfection from me, just the willingness and openness of relationship. What a simple and beautiful truth that is.

When you think of God as Father, what comes to mind?

COMPOSURE

God is the one who saves me;
I will trust him and not be afraid.

ISAIAH 12:2 NCV

You will sleep like a baby, safe and sound—
your rest will be sweet and secure.
You will not be subject to terror, for it will not terrify you.
Nor will the disrespectful be able to push you aside,
because God is your confidence in times of crisis,
keeping your heart at rest in every situation.

PROVERBS 3:24-26 TPT

Give your burdens to the LORD, and he will take care of you.

PSALM 55:22 NLT

If people's thinking is controlled by the sinful self, there
is death. But if their thinking is controlled by the Spirit,
there is life and peace.

ROMANS 8:6 NCV

Lord, may all the conviction in my heart be rooted in you and your unchanging nature. You faithfully follow through with everything you said you would do. Your promises will be fulfilled; every intention that you have set forth into this world will find its place. When I don't know what to hold onto, I hold onto you. Though I am confident in my own abilities to a point, I am incredibly limited in my scope of capability. But with you, nothing is impossible.

When I look at my life and see the question marks over my future, I know that they are not questions to you. You see the end from the beginning and know just what choices will be made along the way. I know that your intentions for me are good. You are not worried about what will come. May my heart rest in the confidence of your mercy and unfailing love that is present with me in every moment along the way. There is no need to give into fear when you are my constant companion and wise guide.

How can you remain steady when it feels like your world is crumbling around you?

CONFIDENCE

I can do everything through Christ,
who gives me strength.

PHILIPPIANS 4:13 NLT

Be my rock of refuge,
to which I can always go;
give the command to save me,
for you are my rock and my fortress....
For you have been my hope, Sovereign LORD,
my confidence since my youth.

PSALM 71:3, 5 NIV

Perfect, absolute peace surrounds those
whose imaginations are consumed with you;
they confidently trust in you.

ISAIAH 26:3 TPT

Do not throw away your confidence,
which has a great reward.

HEBREWS 10:35 NCV

All-powerful God, you hold me together when it feels like everything is falling apart. What a comfort it is to know that nothing worries you; you don't ever get discouraged by the things that overwhelm me. You hem me in with your goodness, surrounding me with your peace that fills me with quiet confidence.

Why would I turn to anything or anyone else for peace when you are the only one who is perfect in love? You don't have ulterior motives hidden in your mercy and you never manipulate or seek to control me. Thank you for your generous love. You are the only God for me! You are the only sure thing in this world; you never change, and you never will. Sustain and heal me in your complete compassion.

How do you find your confidence?

CONSOLATION

You, O Lord, are a shield about me,
My glory, and the One who lifts my head.

PSALM 3:3 NASB

Blessed be the Lord,
Because He has heard the voice of my supplication.
The Lord is my strength and my shield;
My heart trusts in Him, and I am helped;
Therefore my heart exults,
And with my song I shall thank Him.

PSALM 28:6-7 NASB

He did rescue us from mortal danger,
and he will rescue us again.
We have placed our confidence in him,
and he will continue to rescue us.

2 CORINTHIANS 1:10 NLT

God my strength, you see me in my weakness and in my thriving. You don't ever withhold your hand of comfort from me when I need it. You are so much better than the consolation I find in the world. When I am surrounded by community and am drawing strength from them, what a beautiful glimpse it is into the way you work. When I feel isolated, would you surround me with the embrace of your presence that leaves no pain untouched?

Whether I am feeling good about the day or I am just longing for it to be over with, I know that you are the same through it all. You are constant in love and consistent in kindness. May my heart find the strength it needs today to hold onto hope. May I be filled with your peace that brings clarity to every situation. You are the driving force of my life. When I am connected to you, I lack nothing.

How have you been consoled by God in your moments of grief?

CONTENTMENT

To enjoy your work and to accept your lot in life—that is
indeed a gift from God. The person who does that will
not need to look back with sorrow on his past, for God
gives him joy.

ECCLESIASTES 5:20 TLB

I know what it is to be in need, and I know what it is to
have plenty. I have learned the secret of being content
in any and every situation, whether well fed or hungry,
whether living in plenty or in want. I can do all this
through him who gives me strength.

PHILIPPIANS 4:12-13 NIV

Those that the LORD has rescued will return.
They will enter Zion with singing;
everlasting joy will crown their heads.
Gladness and joy will overtake them,
and sorrow and sighing will flee away.

ISAIAH 35:10 NIV

Lord God, your wisdom is above my own understanding. As I meditate on your Word, my heart aligns with your truth that is higher than the laws that hold the universe together. You never overlook a detail, and you never miss an opportunity to extend your mercy. Let my heart rest in your peace today, trusting that you won't forget to fulfill every promise you have made.

Your faithfulness is more reliable than the rising and ebbing of the tides; your love is more loyal than the sunrise. When I consider the seasons of the earth and the way nature responds to the shifts, I can't help but hope for the fruit-bearing seasons to hurry up. Give my heart proper perspective that I wouldn't despise the decay of autumn or the dormancy of winter. In all things, and through all seasons, your love is constant and close.

How can you practice contentment in waiting?

COURAGE

Be strong in the Lord and in his mighty power.
Put on the full armor of God,
so that you can take your stand
against the devil's schemes.

EPHESIANS 6:10-11 NIV

Be alert. Continue strong in the faith.
Have courage, and be strong. Do everything in love.

1 CORINTHIANS 16:13-14 NCV

Even though I walk through the darkest valley,
I will not be afraid. You are with me.
Your shepherd's rod and staff comfort me.

PSALM 23:4 NIRV

"This is my command—be strong and courageous!
Do not be afraid or discouraged.
For the LORD your God is with you wherever you go."

JOSHUA 1:9 NLT

Almighty God, you see what is before me right now. You know the intricacies of what I'm facing. I take hope in the reality that you see it all and you're not worried. You are full of wisdom and strategies for my life. You are master rebuilder and restorer, and I don't need to fix anything on my own. I know that when I look to you, my heart will find the confidence it's looking for.

My heart falters when I forget your unfailing love and your unchanging goodness. Lead me back to you again when I start to be overwhelmed by tough circumstances. Your peace is always available as my portion, and I freely receive from you today. Holy Spirit, fill me with the liquid love of your presence. You are my hope, my strength, and my shield; may my heart take courage in you today.

When was the last time you asked God for courage?

DELIVERANCE

I waited patiently for the LORD;
he turned to me and heard my cry.
He lifted me out of the slimy pit,
out of the mud and mire;
he set my feet on a rock
and gave me a firm place to stand.
He put a new song in my mouth,
a hymn of praise to our God.
Many will see and fear the LORD;
and put their trust in him.

PSALM 40:1–3 NIV

Humble yourselves in the sight of the Lord,
and He will lift you up.

JAMES 4:10 NKJV

Hope of the nations, you are the fulfillment of the longing of every heart. You did not leave your people to struggle and strive through this life on their own; neither do you leave me. You have said that you will never leave or abandon your people. As your child, I hold onto this promise like a thirsty soul to a source of fresh water. You are the living water that washes over me, making me pure and not lacking any good thing.

Lord, how I long to see your goodness revealed in my present circumstances. Knit my heart together with yours, that your love would be stitched into my being. My great expectation isn't my deliverance, though you are faithful to deliver. My great expectation is in your faithfulness in all aspects; you are better than anything I could wrap my hands around. Fill me again with hope.

What do you need God to deliver you from today?

DEPRESSION

Why am I so sad? Why am I so upset?
I should put my hope in God
and keep praising him.

PSALM 42:11 NCV

You, O LORD, are a shield about me, my glory,
and the lifter of my head.

PSALM 3:3 ESV

He has delivered us from the power of darkness and
conveyed us into the kingdom of the Son of His love.

COLOSSIANS 1:13 NKJV

"I am Yahweh, your mighty God!
I grip your right hand and won't let you go!
I whisper to you:
'Don't be afraid; I am here to help you!'"

ISAIAH 41:13 TPT

Holy God, you are the strong fortress that I run into in the storms of life. You are my shield and my protection; you have saved me with your faithful love. When I am tempted to go my own way and forge a path in the wilderness thinking I know best, would you redirect me to your path of life that is already present? You are what I need in every season; you are the wisdom I need to make decisions, the hope I need in the darkness of night, and the love that assures me of my intrinsic worth.

Thank you, God, that everything I have need of is found in you. Your presence is my source of life itself. When I am beaten down by the worries of this world, dragged down by the expectations of failure, and pulled under by waves of depression, would you be my victorious defender, saving me over and over again? I have given you my life, Lord, and I trust you to lead me on in your love.

Can you sense God's comfort and joy in the middle of your sadness?

ENCOURAGEMENT

The LORD your God is with you;
the mighty One will save you.
He will rejoice over you. You will rest in his love;
he will sing and be joyful about you.

ZEPHANIAH 3:17 NCV

Encourage one another daily,
as long as it is called "Today."

HEBREWS 3:13 NIV

Kind words are like honey—
sweet to the soul and healthy for the body.

PROVERBS 16:24 NLT

Be joyful. Grow to maturity. Encourage each other.
Live in harmony and peace.
Then the God of love and peace will be with you.

2 CORINTHIANS 13:11 NLT

Compassionate One, you are full of love, comfort, and encouragement. Oh, how my soul longs for each of those today! Shower me with your affection, surround me with your comfort, and fill me with reassurance. As I am met with the fullness of your goodness, I have more than enough to offer others. I will not hoard your love when you freely offer it. As I give to others, I know that I will receive more because you are a well that never runs dry.

Where I have felt disconnected and alone, may I be met with your love that connects and unifies. You are always better than I expect you to be; when I see the ways you provide, my heart is overcome with gratitude. May today be one for the books in the way that your love shows up. I won't overlook the extravagance of your kindness or keep it to myself.

How can you encourage someone today?

ETERNITY

We are citizens of heaven,
where the Lord Jesus Christ lives.
And we are eagerly waiting
for him to return as our Savior.

PHILIPPIANS 3:20 NLT

"If I go and prepare a place for you, I will come back and
take you to be with me that you also may be where I am."

JOHN 14:3 NIV

That will happen in a flash, as quickly as you can wink an
eye. It will happen at the blast of the last trumpet. Then the
dead will be raised to live forever. And we will be changed.

1 CORINTHIANS 15:52 NIRV

Surely your goodness and love will be with me all my life,
and I will live in the house of the LORD forever.

PSALM 23:6 NCV

Everlasting God, you have brought me out of darkness into the light. In your Word, you promise that where there is destruction, there will be renewal. You make all things new. I trust you to continue to do that in my life and in the world around me. I can't pretend that death's sting isn't still poignant. The pain of loss and separation from those I love is an awful thing to live with. But even in that, there is hope.

Where you are, there is restoration. I trust that you won't let me be lost to the sorrow that fills me when I remember the gaps that missing loved ones have left. You don't expect me to get over it—that's not how love works. But you do promise to be with me in it. Your companionship is my sweet and steady support. And when I, too, pass on from this life into eternity, there will be no more heartbreak. Restored relationships await. May this be a comfort to my heart and a balm to my soul.

Does the thought of eternal life bring you fear or peace?

FAITH

Through Christ you have come to trust in God. And you
have placed your faith and hope in God because he raised
Christ from the dead and gave him great glory.

1 PETER 1:21 NLT

"If you have faith as small as a mustard seed, it is enough.
You can say to this mountain, 'Move from here to there.'
And it will move. Nothing will be impossible for you."

MATTHEW 17:20 NIRV

The important thing is faith—
the kind of faith that works through love.

GALATIANS 5:6 NCV

Faith is confidence in what we hope for
and assurance about what we do not see.

HEBREWS 11:1 NIV

Holy One, I have heard of your goodness and the ways in which you treat your children. You are kind, tenderhearted, and patient in compassion. You are powerful beyond measure, healing the sick and raising the dead. You are relentless in your rescue, always meeting those who call on you with your powerful defense. You don't turn away a curious heart, and you never require what can't be given.

God, you are perfect in love; meet me with the power of your presence. Change my life so I will never be the same again. I don't want to follow an ideology. Come closer, Lord, and transform me from the inside out. Let my vague optimism be turned to confident hope as you reveal yourself in my life. I trust that you won't leave me to endlessly wonder. You are better than that.

Is your faith rooted in a system or in the nature and person of God?

FAITHFULNESS

Your lovingkindness, O LORD, extends to the heavens
Your faithfulness reaches to the skies.

PSALM 36:5 NASB

The Lord is faithful, who will establish you
and guard you from the evil one.

2 THESSALONIANS 3:3 NKJV

LORD, you are my God;
I will exalt you and praise your name,
for in perfect faithfulness
you have done wonderful things,
things planned long ago.

ISAIAH 25:1 NIV

The word of the LORD is upright,
and all his work is done in faithfulness.

PSALM 33:4 ESV

Faithful One, as I recall your kindness in my life—every answered prayer and hope fulfilled—hope breaks through the soil of my heart again. Even in the waiting for your help in my present struggles, I can find your very-present grace in the here and now. Open my eyes to see how big your love is. May my heart expand as your mercy meets me.

As I look to the heavens, my awareness shifts to the greatness of the world around me. My focus is often too small; I can't see the bigger picture when I am focused on one small part of my life. As I lift my eyes, fill my mind with the clarity that a broader perspective brings. Your love knows no limits, and neither can my heart drain your abundant grace. Expand my horizons as I look beyond my limited scope of understanding.

How have you seen the faithfulness of God played out in your life?

FEAR

God gave us his Spirit. And the Spirit doesn't make us
weak and fearful. Instead, the Spirit gives us power
and love. He helps us control ourselves.

2 TIMOTHY 1:7 NIRV

The LORD is my light and my salvation—
whom shall I fear?
The LORD is the stronghold of my life—
of whom shall I be afraid?

PSALM 27:1 NIV

We can say with confidence, "The LORD is my helper,
so I will have no fear. What can mere people do to me?"

HEBREWS 13:6 NLT

When I am afraid, I will trust you.
I praise God for his word.
I trust God, so I am not afraid.
What can human beings do to me?

PSALM 56:3-4 NCV

God, you are the source of all that I need. Truthfully, my heart needs a fresh revelation of that to go deep into my soul. Today, fill me with your faultless love that quells every fear. Quiet my confusion with your perfect peace. You see the true state of my soul and you meet me right where I am in every moment.

Holy Spirit, I rely on you to bring light to my heart and mind. You are the wisdom and peace giver. In you, I find clarity in understanding and in trusting when I can't make any sense of what is going on. Don't let me give up hope, Lord, but draw nearer than the very air I breathe. Thank you for your mercy that is always available; you forever meet me with your compassion.

What fears can you give to God right now?

FORGIVENESS

He is so rich in kindness and grace that he purchased our
freedom with the blood of his Son and forgave our sins.

EPHESIANS 1:7 NLT

As far as the east is from the west,
So far has He removed our transgressions from us.

PSALM 103:12 NASB

If we confess our sins, He is faithful and just to forgive us
our sins and to cleanse us from all unrighteousness.

1 JOHN 1:9 NKJV

"Her sins—and they are many—have been forgiven,
so she has shown me much love. But a person who is
forgiven little shows only little love."

LUKE 7:47 NLT

"If you forgive other people when they sin against you,
your heavenly Father will also forgive you."

MATTHEW 6:14 NIV

Merciful Father, may my life be aligned with your heart of love. As you have forgiven me, may my heart also choose to pardon those who have wronged and hurt me. I realize that often the offense I feel is hurt that has nothing to do with the other person—it is pressing on a wound from long ago. Help me to know when to forgive and let go and when I should forgive and reconcile. I know that as I follow your example, I will find my way.

Holy Spirit, you are my help in this and all things. I rely on you to lead me in love and understanding. When my heart is struggling to hold onto offense, would you show me the root of it? Heal the heart wounds of my past and give me perspective to be able to let go of the resentment that eats away at my joy. I know that as I choose to follow you in this even when I don't want to, I will find freedom and your goodness awaiting me.

Is there someone who needs your forgiveness today?

FREEDOM

The Lord is the Spirit,
and where the Spirit of the Lord is,
there is freedom.

2 CORINTHIANS 3:17 NIV

My brothers and sisters, you were chosen to be free.
But don't use your freedom as an excuse to live under
the power of sin. Instead, serve one another in love.

GALATIANS 5:13 NIRV

"If the Son sets you free,
you are truly free."

JOHN 8:36 NLT

We have freedom now, because Christ made us free.
So stand strong. Do not change and go back
into the slavery of the law.

GALATIANS 5:1 NCV

Yahweh, you never fail to free your people from what holds them captive. Do it again, Lord. Lead me out of this dark night of the soul into the daybreak of your joy. Your loyal love covers me through every trial and every setback. You never withhold your presence from me, and I know that you surround me even when I can't sense you.

You are my freedom, Lord. Guide me into the fullness of life again. Fill me with peace for today and hope for tomorrow. I know you won't abandon me in the middle of my mess. You are faithful to come through again and again. I lean into your heart of mercy that always flows from a place of abundance. Wash over me. May every chain that keeps me from your fullness fall away in the light of your love.

Where do you need freedom in your life?

FRIENDSHIP

A friend loves you all the time,
and a brother helps in time of trouble.

PROVERBS 17:17 NCV

There are "friends" who destroy each other,
but a real friend sticks closer than a brother.

PROVERBS 18:24 NLT

"Greater love has no one than this: to lay down one's
life for one's friends. You are my friends if you do what
I command…. Instead, I have called you friends, for
everything that I learned from my Father I have made
known to you."

JOHN 15:13-15 NIV

"In everything, do to others
what you would want them to do to you."

MATTHEW 7:12 NIRV

Wonderful Counselor, it is in your mercy that my heart has found its home. It is in your family that I have found strength and comfort to keep going. When I am discouraged and would rather isolate myself, would you remind me of the power of community? I know that you are a perfect parent, and you lead and direct me in your kindness. May my heart be encouraged as I meet kindred spirits who know you and are following you along your path of love.

Give me courage to share my victories and disappointments with those I am journeying along this life with. For those I know that love you and love me, may I be open. May we be like iron sharpening iron, encouraging each other in the faith and in life. Lord, bring to mind who I can connect with about what I'm going through. You are faithful to provide for everything—even friends and family. Thank you for relationship, Lord!

Which reliable and trustworthy friends can you be open with?

GOODNESS

Everything God created is good, and nothing is to be
rejected if it is received with thanksgiving.

1 TIMOTHY 4:4 NIV

Taste and see that the LORD is good.
Oh, the joys of those who take refuge in him!

PSALM 34:8 NLT

I remain confident of this:
I will see the goodness of the LORD
in the land of the living.

PSALM 27:13 NIV

They will tell about the amazing things you do,
and I will tell how great you are.
They will remember your great goodness
and will sing about your fairness.

PSALM 145:6-7 NCV

God of goodness, you are full of kindness today. I come to you with all of my heavy baggage; this is the time to trade it in for your mercy that brings freedom. I won't hold back anything, for I know that what you give in return is so much better. I'm so grateful that there isn't a limit to your love; I need never hesitate to ask you for anything because you always freely give out of the abundance of your kingdom.

When the storms of life are raging and I have no strength of my own, I come to you, Lord. On the darkest days, your light shines as brightly as it ever did. You are the source of all goodness. Why would I try to find satisfaction anywhere else? Here I am, Lord; fill me again with your powerful presence. In you is everything I could ever need.

Where do you see the goodness of God in your life?

GRACE

From his fullness we have all received,

grace upon grace.

JOHN 1:16 NRSV

God gives us even more grace, as the Scripture says,

"God is against the proud,

but he gives grace to the humble."

JAMES 4:6 NCV

Sin is no longer your master,

for you no longer live under the requirements of the law.

Instead, you live under the freedom of God's grace.

ROMANS 6:14 NLT

Christ gave each one of us the special gift of grace,

showing how generous he is.

EPHESIANS 4:7 NCV

Gracious God, overcome me with your goodness today. You are the hope that lifts my soul to trust you over and over again. You are before and behind me; you are all around and you are full of love. My heart needs a fresh touch today. Refresh me in your life-giving presence. Wash over my being with the waterfall of your grace.

Lord, I belong to you. Nothing directs my life but you. I will not be overpowered by the world's ways or by the despair of dashed expectations. You will not let me be restrained by limited logic or held down by other's beliefs about me or my life. You are so much better than my most thrilling moments of clarity, purpose, and freedom. I trust that you have me even in the midst of storms and trials. You are my sure thing; I hold onto you as you hold onto me.

What does God's grace look like in your life?

GRATITUDE

I have not stopped giving thanks for you,
remembering you in my prayers.

EPHESIANS 1:16 NIV

Giving thanks is a sacrifice that truly honors me.
If you keep to my path,
I will reveal to you the salvation of God.

PSALM 50:23 NLT

Rejoice always, pray continually,
give thanks in all circumstances;
for this is God's will for you in Christ Jesus.

1 THESSALONIANS 5:16–18 NIV

Give thanks as you enter the gates of his temple.
Give praise as you enter its courtyards.
Give thanks to him and praise his name.

PSALM 100:4 NIRV

Faithful One, when my life's energy is depleting and I have nothing to offer, I know that you are still all I need. In my weakness, I come to you again. As I recall the wonderful ways you've been attentive to my cries for help, my heart swells with gratitude. I remember. I remember how you were with me in joy-filled days and in the darkest days of my life. You won't stop now; you haven't given up on me. May I not give up on you!

Take care of me with your nurturing presence that heals, restores, and supports. You are so much more than life-sustainer, you are life-giver. Breathe new life where I can see nothing but ashes. Turn my mourning into dancing again. I need you.

What can you thank God for right now?

GRIEF

Those who sow in tears shall reap with shouts of joy.

PSALM 126:5 ESV

Let your steadfast love become my comfort
according to your promise to your servant.

PSALM 119:76 NRSV

"Come to me, all you who are weary and burdened,
and I will give you rest. Take my yoke upon you and learn
from me, for I am gentle and humble in heart,
and you will find rest for your souls."

MATTHEW 11:28-29 NIV

Every valley shall be raised up,
every mountain and hill made low;
the rough ground shall become level,
the rugged places a plain.

ISAIAH 40:4 NIV

God, in you I have found a reliable source of hope. Your unfailing love always follows through on your promises. You are faithful in all your ways, and your kindness knows no boundaries. Where there is chaos and confusion, your peace stills with the clarity of wisdom. Where there is worry about the unknowns of the future, your love settles my heart with confidence in your constant character.

I know that nothing will go to waste. Even my sorrow and suffering will lead to the fruit of goodness. I have to believe that you are sowing your fruit of life and beauty amidst the ashes of the losses I've endured. There is no other way for me but to hope because if I don't have that, I would fall into despair. You are faithful! Your love won't stop working and you won't give up on me. Joy is coming.

Does your heart trust God's timing in the shifting of seasons?

GUIDANCE

Guide me in your truth and teach me,
for you are God my Savior,
and my hope is in you all day long.

PSALM 25:5 NIV

I praise the LORD because he advises me.
Even at night, I feel his leading.
I keep the LORD before me always.
Because he is close by my side,
I will not be hurt.

PSALM 16:7-8

We can make our plans,
but the LORD determines our steps.

PROVERBS 16:9 NLT

Those who are led by the Spirit of God
are children of God.

ROMANS 8:14 NIRV

Savior, you are the leader of my life. In you I find the freedom for which my heart so desperately longs. You guide me into truth as I follow you on your pathway of peace. You are my help when I am lost, my confidence when I am undone, and my covering when I am vulnerable. Let my heart find its rest in you again today as you fight for me.

Let your wisdom be my advisor as I venture in this life. I don't lean on my own understanding today; I yield my ways to yours, knowing that you always see the bigger picture. Where I am likely to fail, even there, your wisdom leads me through. I will keep pressing on and pressing into you as I go about my day. You are my holy help; may my heart take courage in the knowledge that you are with me.

Do you trust God to guide you through uncertainty?

HEALTH

The world and its desires pass away,
but whoever does the will of God lives forever.

1 JOHN 2:17 NIV

Don't be wise in your own eyes.
Have respect for the LORD and avoid evil.
That will bring health to your body.
It will make your bones strong.

PROVERBS 3:7-8 NIRV

I will never forget your commandments,
for by them you give me life.

PSALM 119:93 NLT

A happy heart is like good medicine,
but a broken spirit drains your strength.

PROVERBS 17:22 NCV

Healer, meet me with the power of your presence again today. You have been my sustainer through the storm of loss and sorrow. You have been my redeemer in the depths of the darkest valleys, causing life to grow through the cracks and crags of the stony landscape of grief. You are my restorer, the one who is rebuilding my life from the ruins of broken dreams. Revive my heart in your love.

Lord, you have been my security in the midst of trauma; you have been the foundation of grace beneath my feet. I offer you every place that needs your healing touch. Release your power in my life and align me with your loving intentions for abundance and peace. I won't lose hope, for you have never let go of me or looked away from my suffering.

What healing are you believing God for right now?

HOPE

The LORD is good to those whose hope is in him,
to the one who seeks him.

LAMENTATIONS 3:25 NIV

Hope will never bring us shame. That's because God's
love has poured into our hearts. This happened through
the Holy Spirit, who has been given to us.

ROMANS 5:5 NIRV

God has given both his promise and his oath. These two
things are unchangeable because it is impossible for God
to lie. Therefore, we who have fled to him for refuge can
have great confidence as we hold to the hope that lies
before us. This hope is a strong and trustworthy anchor
for our souls. It leads us through the curtain into God's
inner sanctuary.

HEBREWS 6:18-19 NLT

Lord, today I quiet the noise of my mind as I spend a few uninterrupted moments with you. I set aside the worries and the uncertainties of my heart as I lean into your love right now. I come to you with the reality of my world as it is. I won't try to dress it up or down, but I will let you into it.

There is so much out of my control that I just can't get a hold of right now. I am like a top, spinning. But you are steady and sure; you are a firm foundation. You are faithful to deliver me from the chaos of the storms of life with your love. I depend on you, God; you are the only hope I know to have. You are the only help with a perfect track record. I give up my own notions of what should be done, and I surrender to your perfect ways. Come through again.

When was the last time you quieted your thoughts before the Lord and allowed hope to enter your soul?

IDENTITY

See how very much our Father loves us, for he calls us his children, and that is what we are! But the people who belong to this world don't recognize that we are God's children because they don't know him. Dear friends, we are already God's children, but he has not yet shown us what we will be like when Christ appears. But we do know that we will be like him, for we will see him as he really is.

1 JOHN 3:1-2 NLT

Do everything without grumbling or arguing, so that you may become blameless and pure, "children of God without fault in a warped and crooked generation." Then you will shine among them like stars in the sky as you hold firmly to the word of life.

PHILIPPIANS 2:14-16 NIV

Mighty God, your unfailing love chases me down in every season of life. I am reminded that I have been adopted into a family with God's own name as a stamp of identity. I have been marked by your love. You are my Father, my leader, and my friend. It is almost impossible to understand what this means, but I know that someday I will see it all clearly. When heaven's shores are before me, I will know you fully even as I am already fully known by you. There will be no more mystery, no more pain, and no more anguish.

I am grateful to be found in the light of your kingdom here and now. Shine your revelation on my mind and give peace where there have been anxious questions rising within my chest. Your wisdom is better than my own; I rely on you as you call me out. Thank you for drawing me into your beautiful, welcoming family. May I reflect your compassion as I live for you.

Who do you think God really sees when he looks at you?

INSPIRATION

The precepts of the LORD are right,
giving joy to the heart.
The commands of the LORD are radiant,
giving light to the eyes.

PSALM 19:8 NIV

Your laws are my treasure;
they are my heart's delight.

PSALM 119:111 NLT

The whole Bible was given to us by inspiration from
God and is useful to teach us what is true and to make us
realize what is wrong in our lives; it straightens us out
and helps us do what is right.

2 TIMOTHY 3:16 TLB

Lord God, your guiding principles are perfect, and your instructions always come from a full heart of love. When I remember that you are for me and my good, as well as for the benefit of those around me, I can trust that your teachings are pure and right. As I follow your ways of love, I will find the peace and joy that I long for deep within. Your insight is radiant with hope and will never lead me astray.

Today, I will look to your words of wisdom for direction. I will align my actions with the fruit of your Spirit, which you make abundantly clear in your Word. Where fear has kept me stagnant, your love leads me in freedom. When I don't know which way to go or what decision to make, I will look to you. It is in this place that I will find the keys for life that will enlighten me to make insightful choices.

How do you find inspiration?

JOY

May the God of hope fill you with all joy and peace as you
trust in him, so that you may overflow with hope by the
power of the Holy Spirit.

ROMANS 15:13 NIV

"Don't be sad, because the joy of the LORD
will make you strong."

NEHEMIAH 8:10 NCV

The LORD is my strength and shield.
I trust him with all my heart.
He helps me, and my heart is filled with joy.
I burst out in songs of thanksgiving.

PSALM 28:7 NLT

Always be joyful because you belong to the Lord.
I will say it again. Be joyful!

PHILIPPIANS 4:4 NIRV

Holy One, would your love be the spring in my soul that overflows with joy? I've been running on empty; sadness has seeped the strength of my heart. But you, Lord, are never-ending in kindness and always abundantly offering your perfect love that covers every fear. I know that you don't require me to be anything other than what I am at this moment, yet you instruct me and lead me on in growth. When the healing of my heart feels like a type of dying, may I remember that it is only part of the process. Joy comes in the morning after a long, dark night.

When I'm walking through the darkness, with my hand firmly gripping yours, would you fill me with the underlying joy of your presence that is always with me? When my eyes are searching the horizon for any hint of dawn, lift my eyes to where the stars shine, giving light in the meantime. Let your presence with me be the joy that gives me strength today.

Have you experienced joy in the midst of sorrow?

JUSTICE

He will not break the bruised reed, nor quench the dimly
burning flame. He will encourage the fainthearted, those
tempted to despair. He will see full justice given to all
who have been wronged.

ISAIAH 42:3 TLB

Beloved, do not avenge yourselves,
but rather give place to wrath; for it is written,
"Vengeance is Mine, I will repay," says the Lord.

ROMANS 12:19 NKJV

He will not judge by appearance, false evidence,
or hearsay, but will defend the poor and the exploited.
He will rule against the wicked who oppress them. For he
will be clothed with fairness and with truth.

ISAIAH 11:3–5 TLB

Holy One, you are the righteous judge. You alone are qualified to dole out final verdicts. Your ruling no one can contest. You show mercy to whom you show mercy and you hold accountable those who must be held accountable. It is your job and yours alone. Lord, I release the judgments I have made against those who have wronged me. I let go of the offense I've been holding in my heart toward those who have wielded weapons that have hurt others.

I choose to trust you and your power to save and destroy. It is your job to judge people's hearts; it's certainly not mine. Forgive me for the ways that I've criticized and condemned others without your love in mind. Lord, when it is hard for me to justify releasing responsibility, would you give me a glimpse of your power and your mercy? I know that you are trustworthy. I will choose to let go today and for as long as it takes for justice to occur.

Do you trust God enough to let him deal with those who have hurt and offended you?

LIFE

All praise to God, the Father of our Lord Jesus Christ.
It is by his great mercy that we have been born again,
because God raised Jesus Christ from the dead.
Now we live with great expectation.

1 PETER 1:3 NLT

That faith and that knowledge come from the hope for life
forever, which God promised to us before time began.

TITUS 1:2 NCV

"I am the way and the truth and the life.
No one comes to the Father except through me."

JOHN 14:6 NIRV

The Word gave life to everything that was created,
and his life brought light to everyone.

JOHN 1:4 NLT

Living God, your mercy is astounding in its intensity. You cover every weakness, lift off the shame of every failure, and you bring life to the most barren places. I know that you are overflowing with truth and that your love is stronger than death. Your compassion reaches out and tears down every wall that would keep me from you. In the resurrection of Jesus, every barrier was broken down. There is no more veil that keeps mere humans from God's presence. Your Spirit is with me, breathing life and working in miracle power.

Today, I am reminded of your overwhelming affection that stopped at nothing to pursue uninterrupted fellowship with your people. I am grateful to be known as yours; may my heart be encouraged in your love again today. Flood me with the sheer joy of your presence that sets my feet to dancing. May today be the day that the cocoon of my mourning turns into a dance floor.

What is your favorite part of life?

LONELINESS

"Teach them to obey everything that I have taught you, and
I will be with you always, even until the end of this age."

MATTHEW 28:20 NCV

The LORD is near to all who call on him,
yes, to all who call on him in truth.

PSALM 145:18 NLT

Even if my father and mother abandon me,
the LORD will hold me close.

PSALM 27:10 NLT

"Be strong and courageous. Do not be afraid or terrified
because of them, for the LORD your God goes with you;
he will never leave you nor forsake you."

DEUTERONOMY 31:6 NIV

Constant One, I look to you today for the strength I so desperately need. In your love, reach out and surround me with the peace of your presence. I know that I'm not alone. I'm so grateful to have your Spirit as my constant companion and comfort. You are the wisdom that keeps me in line. I also know that you have created us for community. May I not take for granted the people in my life who love you and love me well.

In my loneliness, may I not be lost in isolation. Help me to reach out for help even if it's just for a listening ear or a word of encouragement. A shared load doesn't feel as heavy; when my pride tries to keep me from asking for help, would you remind me that I was never meant to bear this alone? And when I am in a better place, may I be a willing and compassionate friend to those who need a shoulder or an ear. May I find strength in the camaraderie of community.

Who can you turn to for support in your loneliness?

LOSS

Let your steadfast love become my comfort
according to your promise to your servant.

PSALM 119:76 NRSV

Every valley shall be raised up,
every mountain and hill made low;
the rough ground shall become level,
the rugged places a plain.

ISAIAH 40:4 NIV

LORD, have mercy, because I am in misery.
My eyes are weak from so much crying,
and my whole being is tired from grief.
In my distress, I said,
"God cannot see me!"
But you heard my prayer
when I cried out to you for help.

PSALM 31:9, 22 NCV

Compassionate One, when my soul is crushed by grief, and sorrow is the only emotion I can feel, would you surround me with the embrace of your presence? Comfort me with your kindness and relieve my weeping with your mercy. Give me reprieve from the weight of this sadness. I know that you hear me whenever I call out to you, and you won't delay in helping me.

Meet me with exactly what I need today. Give me grace where I am weak and be the strength that sustains me. Thank you for your constant presence that never abandons me in suffering; you don't need to take a break from the weight of my sadness. You help lift the weight of it as you sit with me. I lean into your love today as I do every day. When I am in anguish, your presence lightens the load. Come closer, Lord.

When you are worn down by grief, have you known the relief of God's comfort?

LOVE

Three things will last forever—faith, hope, and love—
and the greatest of these is love.

1 CORINTHIANS 13:13 NLT

Where God's love is, there is no fear, because God's
perfect love drives out fear. It is punishment that makes
a person fear, so love is not made perfect in the person
who fears.

1 JOHN 4:18 NCV

Fill us with your love every morning.
Then we will sing and rejoice all our lives.

PSALM 90:14 NCV

Let love and faithfulness never leave you;
bind them around your neck,
write them on the tablet of your heart.

PROVERBS 3:3 NIV

Compassionate One, meet me with your mercy again today. Fill me with your love in a fresh way. Just like a shower refreshes and cleans, you refresh me with your Spirit so that I am ready for a new day. With your faithful love as my source for all that I need, I have no lack. Let the song of my heart be one of gratitude and thanksgiving today.

Just as the rains water the earth and cause rapid growth in the growing season, so rain over me with your compassion. May your love soak into the soil of my heart and quench the thirst of my soul. You never withhold your waters of life from anyone who asks to drink, so I know that you won't leave my cup dry. Fill me to overflowing today, that your love would flow out of me like floodwaters over the riverbanks. May today be a day filled with your generous love pouring over, in, and through me.

What dry areas of your heart need love's waters to rain down on?

PATIENCE

Warn those who are lazy.

Encourage those who are timid.

Take tender care of those who are weak.

Be patient with everyone.

1 THESSALONIANS 5:14 NLT

Be like those who through faith and patience
will receive what God has promised.

HEBREWS 6:12 NCV

Be completely humble and gentle;
be patient, bearing with one another in love.

EPHESIANS 4:2 NIV

Anyone who is patient has great understanding. But
anyone who gets angry quickly shows how foolish they are.

PROVERBS 14:29 NIRV

Lord, you know how prone I am to worry about the future. When I look around and see evil being celebrated, my heart sinks in my chest. I don't want to live with no hope to hold onto. So then, I will fix my eyes on you! You are full of mercy to all who look to you; you are the defender of the weak and a comforter to the brokenhearted.

Today, Lord, I will give you all of my anxious thoughts. Calm my mind with your perfect peace that is so much wiser than my understanding. As I trust you, turning my heart toward you moment by moment if necessary, I will find your steady strength is alive in me. Here I am; have your way.

Do you view patience as something
you innately have or as something
that can be learned?

PEACE

"I have told you these things,
so that you can have peace because of me.
In this world you will have trouble.
But be encouraged!
I have won the battle over the world."

John 16:33 NIRV

The Lord gives his people strength.
The Lord blesses them with peace.

Psalm 29:11 NLT

May the Lord of peace himself give you peace at all times
and in every way. The Lord be with all of you.

2 Thessalonians 3:16 NIV

"I am leaving you with a gift—peace of mind and heart.
And the peace I give is a gift the world cannot give.
So don't be troubled or afraid."

John 14:27 NLT

Spirit of God, you always carry peace with your presence.
When my heart begins to tremble with fear, would you
breathe the breeze of your peace that calms anxiety and
brings rest? You don't give your peace to take it away, yet I
know that trials and troubles will threaten to disrupt the
peace I carry. When that happens, may your love flood my
senses, bringing everything back into order.

May my whole being be aligned with your heavenly peace,
love, and joy. Today, where there is doubt, may the peace that
passes understanding cover it. Where there is anxiety, may
perfect love calm every nerve. Where there is despair, may your
joy spring up. You are faithful to follow through; meet me with
everything I need today.

When was the last time you felt true peace?

PERSEVERANCE

In a race all the runners run.
But only one gets the prize.
You know that, don't you?
So run in a way that will get you the prize.

1 CORINTHIANS 9:24-25 NIRV

I have tried hard to find you—
don't let me wander from your commands.

PSALM 119:10 NLT

I have fought the good fight,
I have finished the race,
I have kept the faith.

2 TIMOTHY 4:7 NCV

Let us not become weary in doing good, for at the proper
time we will reap a harvest if we do not give up.

GALATIANS 6:9 NIV

Lord, you know how my heart has longed for your wholeness in my life. It is so easy to get distracted by the things of this world—the quests for success, the acceptance of those I admire, the longings for more and better in almost every area. But you, Lord, are full of goodness right here and now. You don't withhold your powerful presence from my life until I get it all together. In fact, my part in our partnership is so much less responsibility than I imagine. I benefit from your grace that covers my weakness.

You are the giver of life, and you never hesitate in coming in close with your incredible affection. As I wait for the fulfillment of your promises, I have the best gift of all—you! You are with me in every moment, loving me to life over and over again. Waiting becomes sweet when I am connected to you.

What do you feel God is calling you to persevere in right now?

PRAISE

Sing to the LORD a new song,
his praise from the ends of the earth,
you who go down to the sea, and all that is in it,
you islands, and all who live in them.

ISAIAH 42:10 NIV

Praise the LORD from the skies.
Praise him high above the earth.
Praise him, all you angels.
Praise him, all you armies of heaven.
Praise him, sun and moon.
Praise him, all you shining stars.
Praise him, highest heavens
and you waters above the sky.
Let them praise the LORD,
because they were created by his command.

PSALM 148:1-5 NCV

Holy One, when I think about your faithfulness, I can't help but find my heart hoping once again. When I'm all out of my own resources of faith, help me to remember to look at what you have done and are doing in your people around me. Even when I walk through a dark desert, refresh me with springs of your living water. I know the harsh reality of my circumstances will not always look this way. But you are with me through it all.

Lord, encourage my heart in you again today. Your loyal love never lets go of your children. I have to believe that when I look back on this time of my life I will see your goodness even here. You don't let anything go to waste; you will restore everything. Even now, let a melody of gratefulness mixed with hope fill my heart.

What is something specific you can praise God for today?

PRAYER

LORD, in the morning you hear my voice.
In the morning I pray to you. I wait for you in hope.

PSALM 5:3 NIRV

Never stop praying.

1 THESSALONIANS 5:17 NIRV

The LORD does not listen to the wicked,
but he hears the prayers of those who do right.

PROVERBS 15:29 NCV

Come, let us bow down in worship,
let us kneel before the LORD our Maker.

PSALM 95:6 NIV

"When you pray, go away by yourself, shut the door
behind you, and pray to your Father in private. Then your
Father, who sees everything, will reward you."

MATTHEW 6:6 NLT

Present One, you are where all my hopes find their fulfillment. There isn't an unspoken prayer that you haven't heard, nor a longing in my heart that has gone unnoticed. Your capacity is abundantly beyond any I could ever imagine. You counsel in kindness and comfort, and you never leave me to my own devices when I ask for your help.

As I talk to you today, may I find comfort and courage in your Word today that meets me precisely where I am. Enlighten my mind with your truth that causes the embers of faith to blow into flames. You are the one who keeps my heart steady as I walk through the winding road of life. You hold my hand and guide me through the unknown, and I find rest in trust, knowing that you always see clearly. You know the way we're going, and you see everything ahead. Lead on, Lord.

What can you pray about right now?

PROMISES

His divine power has granted to us everything pertaining
to life and godliness, through the true knowledge of Him
who called us by His own glory and excellence.

2 PETER 1:3-4 NASB

Your promises have been thoroughly tested,
and your servant loves them.
My eyes stay open through the watches of the night,
that I may meditate on your promises.

PSALM 119:140, 148 NIV

The LORD always keeps his promises;
he is gracious in all he does.

PSALM 145:13 NLT

All the promises of God in Him are Yes,
and in Him Amen, to the glory of God through us.

2 CORINTHIANS 1:20 NKJV

Lord, you are slow to anger and always rich in love. You give your grace out like candy being thrown from floats in a parade and even much more liberally. There is no end to the abundance of your heart of love and mercy that flows freely at all times. When I forget your goodness, come with a wave of your presence to remind me that you never leave at any moment.

You are faithful in all you do, and you never neglect a single promise that you've made. When my heart dips in distress, show up in your power and lift my perspective to yours that I may see you at work here and now. Do not withhold your peace; it is the calm that settles over my soul, bringing me more comfort than I can express. Faithful One, do not fail me now.

Which promises of God help you see hope in your current situation?

PROTECTION

My God is my rock. I can run to him for safety.
He is my shield and my saving strength,
my defender and my place of safety.
The LORD saves me from those who want to harm me.

2 SAMUEL 22:3 NCV

The LORD keeps you from all harm
and watches over your life.
The LORD keeps watch over you as you come and go,
both now and forever.

PSALM 121:7-8 NLT

We are pushed hard from all sides. But we are not beaten
down. We are bewildered. But that doesn't make us lose
hope. Others make us suffer. But God does not desert us.
We are knocked down. But we are not knocked out.

2 CORINTHIANS 4:8-9 NIRV

Good God, when I'm in the midst of trials and troubles,
you are my protector. You defend me from my enemies and
keep me safe under the covering of your mercy. When I am
outnumbered by difficulties, you rise to my aid and help me.
Let me see your miracle-working power in my life as you
bring clarity to the messes I've made and bring peace to the
chaos. I could never do that on my own, but you specialize in
redeeming terrible situations for my good and benefit.

Where I see no glimpse of goodness in a situation, I trust that
you will weave your mercy into it. When I see no way out, I
rely on you to lead me in your kindness. History doesn't favor
the strong but the brave. May my heart know courage as I
press into you. Keep me steady in your love and I will make it
through anything.

How have you recognized
God's protection over your life?

PROVISION

All scripture is inspired by God and is useful for
teaching, for reproof, for correction, and for training in
righteousness, so that everyone who belongs to God may
be proficient, equipped for every good work.

2 TIMOTHY 3:16–17 NRSV

May he give you the power to accomplish all the good
things your faith prompts you to do.

2 THESSALONIANS 1:11 NLT

We are God's handiwork, created in Christ Jesus to do
good works, which God prepared in advance for us to do.

EPHESIANS 2:10 NIV

"Seek the Kingdom of God above all else, and he will give
you everything you need. So don't be afraid, little flock.
For it gives your Father great happiness
to give you the Kingdom."

LUKE 12:31-32 NLT

Great sustainer, you hold me together in the incubator of your love. You heal every broken part of me and restore what was lost. Though there is so much in life that is outside of my control, there is nothing that is outside of yours. I know that you, Lord, are not a dictator and that you don't rule with strict law and punishment. There is grace to learn and grow, to make mistakes and to change my mind. You are gracious in your guidance, and you have an abundance of wisdom to give to all who seek after it.

When I look at my life and see lack, I know that it is an opportunity to wait on your provision. You have everything I need, and you won't let me waste away without any options. You are so much better than that. In the drought of life, when there never seems to be enough, you are still there. Your heart of generosity doesn't ever change; I know that you will provide for everything I need.

Where do you need God's provision in your life?

PURPOSE

You have been raised up with Christ.
So think about things that are in heaven.
That is where Christ is. He is sitting at God's right hand.

COLOSSIANS 3:1 NIRV

We know that in all things God works for the good of
those who love him, who have been called according to
his purpose.

ROMANS 8:28 NIV

My child, pay attention to my words;
listen closely to what I say.
Don't ever forget my words;
keep them always in mind.

PROVERBS 4:20-21 NCV

It is God who works in you to will and to act
in order to fulfill his good purpose.

PHILIPPIANS 2:13 NIV

God on high, you are weaving a tapestry of your grace through all of creation. I know that my life is not untouched by your love. Today, give me eyes to see where you have been working all along. As I look back on my history with you, let me see your telltale love sewn into the fabric of my story. Even in areas where I had no idea you were paying attention, as I look back I see that you have been taking everything into account.

What a wonderful, attentive God you are. You are intricately involved in my life, weaving every part together into a beautiful masterpiece. I know that you won't let anything I go through go to waste; turn it all around for your glory. In the midst of darkness and heavy sorrow, you will knit your faithful love through it. You are incredible, and your attention to detail is astounding.

How do you feel when you think about God having a special purpose for your life?

RECONCILIATION

We are made right with God by placing our faith in
Jesus Christ. And this is true for everyone who believes,
no matter who we are. For everyone has sinned; we
all fall short of God's glorious standard. Yet God, with
undeserved kindness, declares that we are righteous. He
did this through Christ Jesus when he freed us from the
penalty for our sins.

ROMANS 3:22–24 NLT

We have stopped evaluating others from a human point
of view. At one time we thought of Christ merely from
a human point of view. How differently we know him
now! This means that anyone who belongs to Christ has
become a new person. The old life is gone; a new life has
begun! And all of this is a gift from God, who brought us
back to himself through Christ. And God has given us
this task of reconciling people to him.

2 CORINTHIANS 5:16–18 NLT

Holy One, let every thought that denies your power be brought into alignment with your matchless wonder and worth. You are the miracle maker, the mountain mover, and the God of the impossible. In resurrection life, the power of sin and death was rendered defeated. You made a way where there seemed to be none and at the highest price. Thank you, God, that I am not just a friend of yours—though that would be enough. As a child of the Father of lights, I am a reflection of the same love that risked everything for freedom and unity.

Lord, I invite your power to move in my life in the same way that Jesus was raised to life forever. Bring new life out of the ashes of my life; bring restoration where there is destruction. Redeem that which has been taken from me and breathe hope into the caverns of my heart that await your life-giving light.

Where do you need God's power of reconciliation to move right now?

RELAXATION

Blessed is the one who trusts in the Lord,
whose confidence is in him.
They will be like a tree planted by the water
that sends out its roots by the stream.
It does not fear when heat comes;
its leaves are always green.
It has no worries in a year of drought
and never fails to bear fruit.

JEREMIAH 17:7–8 NIV

Those who love me, I will deliver;
I will protect those who know my name.
When they call to me, I will answer them;
I will be with them in trouble,
I will rescue them and honor them.

PSALM 91:14-15 NRSV

Lord, you see the heaviness of my heart and the grief that saps every reserve of strength. When I have nothing to give, you don't require more from me. You come in close with your tender presence, and you surround me with your peace. In the middle of my loss, you sit with me. You are the hand that holds me together when I am falling apart.

My attempts in life to accomplish things fade quickly when the reality of loss hits me like a tsunami. My inner world is in wreckage—I don't even know where to look! But there you are, right in the middle of my chaos, somehow bringing order with your peaceful presence. I don't need to do anything but rest in you right now. Come again, Lord, and hold me close in your love. I choose to let everything go and rest in you.

How can you practice relaxing in God's presence?

RELIABILITY

"All people are like grass.
All their glory is like the flowers in the field.
The grass dries up. The flowers fall to the ground.
But the word of the LORD lasts forever."

1 PETER 1:24-25 NIRV

Every good action and every perfect gift is from God. These
good gifts come down from the Creator of the sun, moon,
and stars, who does not change like their shifting shadows.

JAMES 1:17 NCV

You are near, LORD,
and all your commands are true.
Long ago I learned from your statutes
that you established them to last forever.

PSALM 119:151-152 NIV

God, you are the ultimate source of peace, hope, and joy. In you, I know that I have everything I need for life and more. You see me in my pursuit, in my questioning and in the areas I feel stuck. Though I change my mind, sometimes daily, you are as constant as the tides of the ocean. However, unlike the tide, you don't rise and fall. You are consistent in compassion and reliable in mercy. When everything else falls away, there you remain with the abundance of your affection.

Lord, keep my heart set on you, even in the midst of temporary disappointments and heartbreak. You are the one thing that I can rely on in this life. I can't depend on myself in the same way. You are unfailing in your goodness and constant in your faithfulness. Thank you for always being a firm foundation I can stand on.

How does it make you feel knowing you can rely on God for everything?

RELIEF

"I am the Alpha and the Omega—
the Beginning and the End.
To all who are thirsty I will give freely
from the springs of the water of life."

REVELATION 21:6 NLT

I prayed to the LORD, and he answered me.
He freed me from all my fears.
Those who look to him for help will be radiant with joy.

PSALM 34:4–5 NLT

The Spirit helps us in our weakness. We do not know
what we ought to pray for, but the Spirit himself
intercedes for us through wordless groans. And he
who searches our hearts knows the mind of the Spirit,
because the Spirit intercedes for God's people in
accordance with the will of God.

ROMANS 8:26–27 NIV

Father of mercy, in my sorrow I let myself come undone in your presence. I couldn't hold myself together if I tried. You are patient to sit with me in my discomfort and hold me close in your compassion. You don't expect me to process the pain I'm experiencing quickly or move on from my sadness rooted in loss. You are the closest comfort I've ever known and relief to my soul.

When you support me with your unfailing affection, the strength of your love keeps me rooted in who you are and in who I am in you. As I am loved to life, even in my darkest moments, I lean into your example of boundless mercy. As I experience it, so will I be able to offer it. I trust that in your time, nothing will have been wasted. Use every bit of this and turn it into beauty beyond my imagining.

What moments of relief have you experienced within your grief?

RESTORATION

He has saved us and called us to a holy life—
not because of anything we have done
but because of his own purpose and grace.

2 TIMOTHY 1:9 NIV

"Let us praise the Lord, the God of Israel,
because he has come to help his people
and has given them freedom.
He has given us a powerful Savior."

LUKE 1:68-69 NCV

We can boldly enter heaven's Most Holy Place because of
the blood of Jesus. By his death, Jesus opened a new and
life-giving way through the curtain into the Most Holy
Place. And since we have a great High Priest who rules
over God's house, let us go right into the presence of God
with sincere hearts fully trusting him.

HEBREWS 10:19—22 NLT

Patient One, your kindness leads me back to you time and time again. Nothing goes wasted in your love; even grief has found a purpose in calling me back to you. In my sorrow, I have no hope for healing or reconciliation on my own. I cannot heal my bleeding heart; I can barely stay conscious in my life for all the sadness seeping out of my soul. But you, Lord, you bind up the brokenhearted. You heal those overcome with the agony of mourning. You do. In the process of grieving, I will not forget that your love is powerful enough to fill every crack and crevice. You won't let me drown in sorrow.

In you there is hope. Hope for life beyond this small, lived existence. Where there is hope, there is light, and where there is light, there is life. I set my eyes on you again today, trusting you to do what only you can do.

In your grief, have you known God's restoration?

REWARD

Work willingly at whatever you do, as though you were
working for the Lord rather than for people. Remember
that the Lord will give you an inheritance as your reward,
and that the Master you are serving is Christ.

COLOSSIANS 3:23-24 NLT

"Love your enemies, do good to them, and lend to them
without expecting to get anything back. Then your
reward will be great, and you will be children of the Most
High, because he is kind to the ungrateful and wicked."

LUKE 6:35 NIV

Even if you suffer for doing what is right,
God will reward you for it.

1 PETER 3:14 NLT

Without faith it is impossible to please God. Those who
come to God must believe that he exists. And they must
believe that he rewards those who look to him.

HEBREWS 11:6 NIRV

Rock of ages, you never change in compassion. Your mercy doesn't rise one day and fall the next. You are consistent in kindness and forever faithful in love. You rise to the defense of those who call on your name, and you surround those who look to you with your unfailing love. There is no time limit to your affection; you are better than the most caring parent this world has ever known.

You are my rock of salvation, my only firm hope. Everything else will pass away, but you never will. You who created the heavens, the earth, and everything within them are the same God who will keep every promise of protection. I follow your faithful leadership, and I know you won't stop guiding me through life. When I've crossed over into eternity, there you will be—my great reward.

How does it make you feel knowing
there is a great reward waiting for you
at the end of this life?

SAFETY

The Lord also will be a refuge for the oppressed,
A refuge in times of trouble.
Those who know Your name will put their trust in You;
For You, Lord, have not forsaken those who seek You.

PSALM 9:9–10 NKJV

I call to you from the ends of the earth when I am afraid.
Carry me away to a high mountain.
You have been my protection,
like a strong tower against my enemies.

PSALM 61:2-3 NCV

"Don't be afraid of anyone,
because I am with you to protect you," says the Lord.

JEREMIAH 1:8 NCV

Holy One, when the storms of life rage and I lose my footing, there you are to catch me and bring me to safety. I hide myself in the safety of your embrace, trusting that you cover me completely. You see my aching heart, and you don't look down on me for being in pain. You come to my rescue and surround me with the healing balm of your presence.

I have no hope apart from you—no confidence in anything of my own or of the world's. You are the only thing that lasts in this world full of passing trends and inevitable decay. You are the same powerful, compassionate God who delivered Daniel from the lion's den and led the Israelites out of captivity. I trust that you won't let me fall, God, and you will get me through everything I face.

Do you feel safe when you
think about God being near you?

SALVATION

"This is how God loved the world: He gave his one and only Son, so that everyone who believes in him will not perish but have eternal life."

JOHN 3:16 NLT

The wages of sin is death, but the gift of God is eternal life in Christ Jesus our Lord.

ROMANS 6:23 NIV

God's grace has saved you because of your faith in Christ. Your salvation doesn't come from anything you do. It is God's gift.

EPHESIANS 2:8 NIRV

If you openly declare that Jesus is Lord and believe in your heart that God raised him from the dead, you will be saved.

ROMANS 10:9 NLT

Gracious God, it is your work in my life that has any lasting effect. My own motivations and strength eventually wane, but yours never do. I'm so thankful that my salvation is not based on my own abilities but on your undying love. I never need to earn your love—you always give it freely. I run again into your arms of grace today. In your arms, I find a safe place to rest. You restore me as I lean into your love.

I have gladly received your gift of life through the grace that you give. I know that all goodness in my life is from you; I won't overlook what you have given me. May my eyes be focused on your kindness, looking for clues of your tender love planted in my life. Give me eyes to see how you are present with me.

How do you respond to the message of salvation?

STRENGTH

God is our refuge and strength,
an ever-present help in trouble.

PSALM 46:1-3 NIV

The Lord is faithful; he will strengthen you
and guard you from the evil one.

2 THESSALONIANS 3:3 NIRV

Don't be afraid, for I am with you.
Don't be discouraged, for I am your God.
I will strengthen you and help you.
I will hold you up with my victorious right hand.

ISAIAH 41:10 NLT

The LORD protects those who truly believe....
All you who put your hope in the LORD
be strong and brave.

PSALM 31:23-24 NCV

Lord, you are the support I need in the struggles of life. You hold me tight, making sure I'm not beyond your grip. You lift me up when I stumble and you set me straight when I am turned around. When worries threaten my peace, remind me again of your steadfast love that never changes.

You are more faithful than the most loyal lover and more attentive than the most involved mother. You are perfect in your leadership and your intentions are as pure as your love. I could not find a better comfort in anyone else, try as I might. Draw near to me today with the power of your presence and let hope break through the soil of my heart once again.

What makes you feel strong?

STRESS

Praise the LORD, my soul;
all my inmost being, praise his holy name.
Praise the LORD, my soul,
and forget not all his benefits—
who forgives all your sins
and heals all your diseases,
who redeems your life from the pit
and crowns you with love and compassion,
who satisfies your desires with good things
so that your youth is renewed like the eagle's.

PSALM 103:1-5 NIV

Commit your actions to the LORD.
and your plans will succeed.

PROVERBS 16:3 NLT

As pressure and stress bear down on me,
I find joy in your commands.

PSALM 119:143 NLT

Father, when I am overcome with emotions that feel like they will sweep me away, you keep me anchored in your love. I offer you every worry and stress; I don't want my hope to be choked out by the vines of anxiety. You come in close with your comfort and surround me with the peace of your presence. I will never find another like you who soothes my soul the way you do.

Lord, draw closer even now. Calm me with your gentle nearness and envelop me in your love. There is nothing that I could ever have need of that you couldn't provide. In your storehouse of abundance, you have more than enough resources for every possibility I will ever face. I rely on you more than I can articulate. Who else is there like you in all the earth? Don't fail me now, Lord; reveal your faithfulness in my life again!

Where do you turn for comfort when you feel stressed out?

SUPPORT

Whom have I in heaven but you?
And earth has nothing I desire besides you.
My flesh and my heart may fail,
but God is the strength of my heart
and my portion forever.

PSALM 73:25–26 NIV

You, God, see the trouble of the afflicted;
you consider their grief and take it in hand.
The victims commit themselves to you;
you are the helper of the fatherless.

PSALM 10:14 NIV

You are my hiding place;
You shall preserve me from trouble;
You shall surround me with songs of deliverance.

PSALM 32:7 NKJV

Comforter, you are the safe place where I find rest for my soul amidst the storms of life. You are the peace that passes all understanding and my true north. With my life hitched to yours, I know that you will keep me on the path that leads to life. You are my refuge, Lord, and my constant source of strength when my own fails.

Again, Lord, I place my trust in you. Every morning is a new opportunity to yield my heart, my hope, and my intentions to your higher wisdom and will. My heart's hopes will be fulfilled in you. Thank you for the reality of your presence with me now and forever. Your love is my support and the force that sustains my life.

When do you feel the most supported by God?

TRUST

Those who know the LORD trust him,
because he will not leave those who come to him.

PSALM 9:10 NCV

I trust in you, LORD. I say, "You are my God."
My whole life is in your hands.
Save me from the hands of my enemies.
Save me from those who are chasing me.

PSALM 31:14-15 NIV

Take delight in the LORD,
and he will give you your heart's desires.
Commit everything you do to the LORD.
Trust him, and he will help you.

PSALM 37:4-5 NLT

Loyal Lord, I'm relying on you to help me. You see my struggles today, and they're too much for me to handle on my own. When I try to fix things and find that I'm in a bigger mess than before, I throw my hands up in surrender. Instead of just giving up, Lord, I let go. Come into this mess and bring your peace that clarifies. You are wiser than I am, and you have infinite resources at your disposal. With your help as my hope, I lean on you. I'm done depending on my own understanding. It may get me so far, but it never follows all the way through.

In your power, Lord, do what only you know how to do and bring new life out of the ashes of devastation. I don't even know where to start; I've done all I can. I trust you because you are trustworthy. You are faithful in follow-through; I'm giving in and resting in you today!

What areas can you trust God with that are out of your control?

TRUTH

"When he, the Spirit of truth, comes,
he will guide you into all the truth."

JOHN 16:13 NIV

The very essence of your words is truth;
all your just regulations will stand forever.

PSALM 119:160 NLT

"If you abide in My word,
you are My disciples indeed.
And you shall know the truth,
and the truth shall make you free."

JOHN 8:31-32 NKJV

Teach me your way, O LORD,
that I may walk in your truth;
unite my heart to fear your name.

PSALM 86:11 ESV

Mighty God, in you is the light of life. I drink up your presence like one whose thirst has not been quenched in far too long. I have been running dry more often than I'd like to admit; sadness has seeped me of my strength. But you, Lord, are an ever-flowing fountain of love to all who call on you. I don't need to beg for my portion; you always give freely and generously.

Lord, fill me with the wisdom of your ways. You give revelation to make your truths evident in the simplest of terms. You have solutions for every complex problem, and your answers are not hard to decipher. May my heart understand and my mind comprehend what you are saying today. As I follow your guidelines to life, I will find the keys that I have been looking for.

What steps can you take to align yourself with God's truth?

UNDERSTANDING

Understanding is like a fountain of life
to those who have it.

PROVERBS 16:22 NIRV

The teaching of your word gives light,
so even the simple can understand.

PSALM 119:130 NLT

Give me understanding,
so that I may keep your law and obey it with all my heart.

PSALM 119:34 NIV

Those who love your teachings will find true peace,
and nothing will defeat them.

PSALM 119:165 NCV

Don't act thoughtlessly, but understand
what the Lord wants you to do.

EPHESIANS 5:17 NLT

Wise One, your perspective is perfect. You see and know everything there is to know; there are no mysteries to you. Why would I rely on my own inadequate understanding when I have access to your unmatched wisdom? I won't be swept away by the theories of proud people; I test everything according to your Word that guides me. The fruit of wisdom is life and peace.

May my heart rest in trust as you guide me along the path of life. You lead me in love and understanding, and my own will grow as I spend time getting to know you more. A lifetime spent knowing and being known by you is one well lived. May I remember that when I start to get tripped up by the rises and dips of success and failure. In every moment, may I find my purpose in you, God. Let all lesser things fade into the background.

How do you seek to understand
God's will each day?

VICTORY

You can prepare a horse for the day of battle.
But the power to win comes from the LORD.

PROVERBS 21:31 NIRV

Every child of God defeats this evil world,
and we achieve this victory through our faith.

1 JOHN 5:4 NLT

Say to the anxious and fearful,
"Be strong and never afraid.
Look, here comes your God!
He is breaking through to give you victory!
He comes to avenge your enemies.
With divine retribution he comes to save you!"

ISAIAH 35:4 TPT

"The LORD your God is the one who goes with you to fight
for you against your enemies to give you victory."

DEUTERONOMY 20:4 NIV

Victorious One, in you is every triumph. When it seems as though all is hopeless and there is no path for peace, you somehow make a way and redeem every situation. Someday, with unveiled eyes, I will see it all plainly as you see it all. For now, I trust that you have not given up or given in. You are still faithful to your promises.

You haven't failed, and if it looks like you have, I know it isn't the end! You always come through with redemption and resurrection power. Always. I hang on to you and trust that you are fighting for me in ways that I can't bring myself to ask. I am not alone in any battle. Fill me now with your broader perspective and the presence of your love that quells every fear.

As a child of God, what does victory look like in your life?

WHOLENESS

He will take our weak mortal bodies and change them
into glorious bodies like his own, using the same power
with which he will bring everything under his control.

PHILIPPIANS 3:21 NLT

Celebrate with praises the God and Father of our Lord
Jesus Christ, who has shown us his extravagant mercy.
For his fountain of mercy has given us a new life—we are
reborn to experience a living, energetic hope through
the resurrection of Jesus Christ from the dead. We are
reborn into a perfect inheritance that can never perish,
never be defiled, and never diminish. It is promised
and preserved forever in the heavenly realm for you!
Through our faith, the mighty power of God constantly
guards us until our full salvation is ready to be revealed
in the last time.

1 PETER 1:3–5 TPT

Lord, you know how my heart has longed for your wholeness in my life. It is so easy to get distracted by the things of this world—the quests for success, the acceptance of those I admire, the longings for more and better in almost every area. But you, Lord, are full of goodness right here and now. You don't withhold your powerful presence from my life until I get it all together. In fact, my part in our partnership is so much less responsibility than I imagine. I benefit from your grace that covers my weakness.

You are the giver of life, and you never hesitate in coming in close with your incredible affection. As I wait for the fulfillment of your promises, I have the best gift of all—you! You are with me in every moment, loving me to life over and over again. Waiting becomes sweet when I am connected to you.

How does understanding eternal wholeness benefit you in this life?

WISDOM

Wisdom will come into your mind,
and knowledge will be pleasing to you.
Good sense will protect you;
understanding will guard you
It will keep you from the wicked,
from those whose words are bad.

PROVERBS 2:10-12 NCV

If any of you needs wisdom, you should ask God for it.
He will give it to you. God gives freely to everyone and
doesn't find fault.

JAMES 1:5 NIRV

My brothers and sisters, I am sure that you are full of
goodness. I know that you have all the knowledge you
need and that you are able to teach each other.

ROMANS 15:14 NCV

Wise One, you are full of wisdom for every situation. When confusion blurs my thoughts, your truth is the light that burns off the fog of chaos. You bring order to the mess of my swirling emotions, and you set everything in its right place in your higher understanding.

When I see from your perspective, I know that I will comprehend more than I can from my limited view. You see every detail as a part of a bigger whole. Lord, I submit my heart to you again, trusting in your wisdom to guide me into life and restoration. Even when I don't understand the workings as I walk in your way, I will trust that you always lead in love and for my ultimate good.

Do you trust that God's ways
are full of wisdom and love?

WORRY

Turn your worries over to the LORD.
He will keep you going.
He will never let godly people be shaken.

PSALM 55:22 NIRV

"Who of you by worrying
can add a single hour to your life?"

LUKE 12:25 NIV

Worry weighs a person down;
an encouraging word cheers a person up.

PROVERBS 12:25 NLT

Do not worry about anything, but pray and ask God for
everything you need, always giving thanks. And God's
peace, which is so great we cannot understand it,
will keep your hearts and minds in Christ Jesus.

PHILIPPIANS 4:6-7 NCV

King of kings, I belong to you. I have yielded my life to yours, with your Spirit as my guide. You lead me through the wilderness of this life with patience and strength. You tenderly steer me back onto the path of life when I begin to stray. My life is firmly rooted in yours, and the fruit that it bears will reflect the source I'm connected to.

God, I will not fear even in the midst of famine. You are my supply in every season, in every step, at every point in my life. And when do feel distress in my heart, I invite you into it. I know that your love is stronger than any worry or doubt that may crop up. You are bigger than the unknowns of this life; you are more faithful than the rising sun. Fill my life with the fruit of your goodness even in the wasteland.

Can you lay your worries aside and trust that God is always good?

BroadStreet Publishing Group, LLC.
Savage, Minnesota USA
Broadstreetpublishing.com

Prayers & Promises for Grief and Loss

© 2020 by BroadStreet Publishing®

978-1-4245-6103-2 (faux)
978-1-4245-6104-9 (ebook)

Design by Chris Garborg | garborgdesign.com
Compiled and edited by Michelle Winger | literallyprecise.com

Printed in China.

20 21 22 23 24 25 26   7 6 5 4 3 2 1